Healthy Habits

Panda's Guide to Mental Well-Being

Published in 2026 by Windmill Books,
an Imprint of Rosen Publishing
2544 Clinton St.
Buffalo, NY 14224

First published in Great Britain in 2023 by Hodder & Stoughton

Credits
Commissioning editor: Sarah Peutrill
Series editor: Lisa Edwards
Series Designer: Rachel Lawston

Cataloging-in-Publication Data
Names: Edwards, Lisa, author. | Roberts, Sian, illustrator.
Title: Panda's guide to mental well-being / Lisa Edwards, illustrated by Sian Roberts.
Description: Buffalo, NY : Windmill Books, 2026. | Series: Healthy habits
Identifiers: ISBN 9781538399675 (pbk.) | ISBN 9781538399682 (library bound) |
ISBN 9781538399699 (ebook)
Subjects: LCSH: Mental health--Juvenile literature. | Pandas--Juvenile literature.
Classification: LCC RA790.E393 2026 | DDC 616.89--dc23

Printed in the United States of America

CPSIA Compliance Information: Batch #CSWM26
For Further Information contact Rosen Publishing at 1-800-237-9932

Healthy Habits

Panda's Guide to Mental Well-Being

Lisa Edwards

Siân Roberts

WINDMILL BOOKS™

Panda and her cub are happily playing together.
Little Panda loves to roll around on the forest floor.

What do you do that makes you feel happy?
Feeling happy means that your mind is healthy.

Panda knows that milk, bamboo shoots, and leaves are good for Little Panda. Pandas eat for up to fourteen hours every day!

When your body is filled with healthy food, you feel good. Make sure you eat a healthy breakfast like Little Panda!

Little Panda is learning how to climb by practicing on Mom.
One day he will climb up a tree all by himself!

Learning new things like how to ride a bike, play a musical instrument, or build something can be lots of fun.

After his climbing lesson, Little Panda goes in the water with his mom for the first time. When he is older he will be able to swim and splash around.

Playing a game or taking part in a sport
you love will make you feel good.

Panda and her cub settle down for their first sleep of the day. It's been a tiring morning!

If you get enough sleep - 9 to 12 hours - you will feel good the next day. Going to bed at the same time every day helps you to sleep properly.

Panda and her cub wake up in the evening for their second meal of the day.

It's important to have a routine - things that you do every day at the same time, like exercise, having a meal, or reading a story. They help your mind stay healthy.

Panda and her cub talk to each other using sounds we find hard to hear. They are very quiet animals most of the time.

If you are worried about something, it's a good idea to talk to someone about it.

Little Panda has spotted Snow Leopard nearby. Panda reassures him that she is just a mom too, quietly looking after her baby.

It's a good idea to tell the truth when something is worrying you. Your mind can rest when your worry is shared with someone.

Being kind to other people
makes us feel good.
We can help others and
share what we have.

Panda sometimes shares
her food with other
animals if they need it.

Being kind to yourself is important.
If you feel upset or sad about something,
take time alone to breathe slowly.

Panda is happiest on her own with her cub, walking through the forest looking for fresh bamboo to eat.

Panda does not become angry with other animals who come near her home and cub. Instead, she moves away.

If you feel angry with someone, it's a good idea to move away until you feel calm and able to talk nicely to them.

When they do meet each other, pandas often sit or play together in silence.

Spending time with others can make you feel happy.

As they settle down for another nap, Little Panda says thank you to his mom for a lovely day. He gives her a big hug.

When you feel grateful for the good
things in your life, you feel happy.
What do you feel thankful for?

Panda has been showing us how she looks after her and her cub's mental wellbeing. How can you look after yours?

Do things that make you feel happy

Eat healthy food

Learn how to do something new

Make sure you exercise

Get enough sleep

Stick to a routine

If something is worrying you, talk about it

Tell the truth

Be kind to others

Be kind to yourself

Spend time with others

Be thankful for what you have

Glossary

Bamboo a type of tall grass with hard, hollow stems.

Grateful feeling thankful for something.

Healthy a healthy body or mind means it is working well and feeling good. Food or exercise that is good for your body and mind is also said to be healthy.

Reassure to say or do something to make someone feel better.

Red Panda a small animal that lives in the mountains of Asia.

Routine an order of doing several things, such as brushing your teeth before you go to bed.

Snow Leopard a type of big cat that lives in the mountains of Asia.

Let's talk about healthy habits...

The *Healthy Habits* series has been written to help young children begin to understand how they can live healthy lives, both in their relationships with others and in their own bodies.

It provides a starting point for parents, caregivers, and teachers to discuss healthy ways of being in the world with little learners. The series involves a cast of animal characters who behave in healthy ways in their own habitats, relating their experiences to familiar, everyday scenarios for children.

Panda's Guide to Mental Wellbeing

This story looks at all the ways you can keep your mind healthy.

The book aims to encourage a child's awareness of the importance of eating well and getting enough exercise and sleep to mental wellbeing. It offers children a simple checklist of activities that they can use to keep their minds happy and healthy.

How to use the book:

The book is designed for adults to share with either an individual child, or a group of children, and as a starting point for discussion.

Choose a time when the children are relaxed and have time to share the story.

Before reading the story:

- Spend time looking at the illustrations and talking about what the book might be about before reading it together. Ask the children to look at the details in each picture to see what all the creatures are doing – some of them are echoing the main themes in the background of the story.
- Encourage children to employ a "phonics-first" approach to tackling new words by sounding them out.

After reading the story:

- Talk about the story with the children. Ask the children to list occasions when they have felt sad and the reasons why. What were they doing when they felt sad?
- Ask them to list occasions when they have felt happy and the reasons why. What were they doing when they felt happy?
- Place the children into groups and ask half of them to create a healthy daily routine based on Panda's. Ask the other groups to list all the things they feel grateful for in one day.
- At the end of the session, discuss a healthy daily routine with the whole class and talk about how feeling thankful can make our minds happier and healthier. Finish by discussing all the ways being kind to others and ourselves can contribute to our mental wellbeing.